ON THE SAVANNAH

Written By
Emilie Dufresne

BookLife PUBLISHING

©2020
BookLife Publishing Ltd.
King's Lynn
Norfolk PE30 4LS

All rights reserved.
Printed in Malaysia.

A catalogue record for this book is available from the British Library.

ISBN: 978-1-83927-837-2

Written by:
Emilie Dufresne

Edited by:
Robin Twiddy

Designed by:
Danielle Rippengill

All facts, statistics, web addresses and URLs in this book were verified as valid and accurate at time of writing. No responsibility for any changes to external websites or references can be accepted by either the author or publisher.

Sniff! Sniff!

Sniff! Sniff!

Image Credits

All images are courtesy of Shutterstock.com, unless otherwise specified. With thanks to Getty Images, Thinkstock Photo and iStockphoto. Front Cover – PremiumVector, ainahart, Svietlieisha Olena, Iterum, YevO, Iron 2016, Valeri Hadeev. Title typeface used throughout – PremiumVector. 2 – STUDIO 11. 4 – Elina Litovkina, robuart. 5 – toowaret. 6&7 – BigBoom. 6 – lukpedclub. 7 – Anan Kaewkhammul, Eric Isselee, Iakov Filimonov. 8 – Sergey Uryadnikov. 9 – Mogens Trolle, vectortatu. 10&11 – John Ceulemans. 11 – a_v_d, Eric Isselee, Iakov Filimonov. 12 – J. NATAYO. 13 – Marie Lemerle, GraphicsRF. 14&15 – TaTum2003, Shanvood. 15 – Anan Kaewkhammul, John Kasawa, Susan Schmitz. 16 – dirkr, Ekaterina_Mikhaylova. 17 – robuart, David Gallaher. 18&19 – KAMONRAT. 19 – Eric Isselee, Iakov Filimonov, Valdis Skudre. 20 – Aspen Photo, puaypuay. 21 – This Is Me, passengerz, MaryValery. 22 – Cristina Romero Palma, Neil Bromhall. 23 – FJAH.

CONTENTS

Page 4   All About Poo

Page 6   Showered in Splats

Page 10   White and Chalky

Page 14   Magnificent Mounds

Page 18   Dozens of Drops

Page 22   Bonus Poo!

Page 24   Glossary and Index

*Words that look like **this** can be found in the glossary on page 24.*

ALL ABOUT POO

You do it. Your teacher does it. Even the worms in the ground do it. Everybody poos! But have you ever seen a poo and wondered who did it?

Let's look around the <u>savannah</u> and see whose poo we can find.

Don't touch any poo you find on the savannah. Poo has lots of nasty things in it!

On the next page you will see some poo found on the savannah. Learn about the poo and then choose which of the three animals you think made the mess!

SHOWERED IN SPLATS

What's that lumpy cloud in the water? Is it... poo?

This poo is showered across the land and water for metres around.

The poo is a green-brown colour. This animal probably eats a lot of <u>vegetation</u>.

WHOSE POO WAS IT?

It was the hippopotamus's POO!

It was me! Stand back, I can feel another one coming.

Male hippopotamuses use their tails like a propeller to fling their poo as far as they can. This helps them to mark their territory.

Hippos spend a lot of the hot savannah days wallowing (and pooing!) in the water to keep cool.

Sometimes, hippos poo so much while wallowing that it kills the fish in the water.

SPLATTER ZONE

WHITE AND CHALKY

Wow – I've never seen a poo like that!

There are lots of poos all done in one mound as though this area is used as a communal toilet.

The white colour means there is lots of calcium in the poo.

Whose poo could this be? Choose which of these three animals you think did it.

Hyena

If this area is used as a communal toilet, the animal probably lives in a **pack**.

This poo really stands out on the grassy savannah.

Sorry, did you say my name?

Aardvark

You think I did what...?

Giraffe

WHOSE POO WAS IT?

It was the hyena's POO!

Hey! It wasn't just me. The whole pack pooed there...

Hyenas are **carnivores** and scavengers which means they eat animals and sometimes the leftovers from other carnivores.

QUEUE HERE

The communal toilets help hyenas mark their territory.

Hurry up, Henry – I need a number two!

Hyenas have extremely sharp teeth that let them eat the bones of their **prey**.

Any extra calcium left over from eating bones comes out in their poo, making it white.

MAGNIFICENT MOUNDS

What a mighty poo we have here!

There are lots of insects feeding from the poo.

This poo has lots of grass in it. This animal is probably a <u>herbivore</u>.

WHOSE POO WAS IT?

It was the elephant's POO!

It was me! I made the mound of poo!

An elephant spends around 15 hours a day eating and can eat around 150 kilograms of vegetation in that time! That's about the same as ten bales of hay!

Elephants may eat a lot, but they don't digest it very well. In fact, around half of the food they eat goes through them undigested.

This means that their poo still has lots of good things in it that other animals like to eat.

Baby elephants sometimes eat their mother's poo to get important <u>bacteria</u> in their bodies.

Thanks, Mum!

DOZENS OF DROPS

Look at this impressive pile of droppings! Whose poo could it be?

The poo is very smooth and it is full of well-chewed vegetation. This animal is probably a herbivore.

The droppings are the size of grapes. They are flat on one side as though they were squished when they fell to the ground.

WHOSE POO WAS IT?

It was the giraffe's POO!

I spend around 20 hours of my day eating leaves. All that food has to come out somewhere!

Giraffes have tongues that are half a metre long. That's around the same length as a cat. Their tongue helps them reach the tallest leaves on the trees.

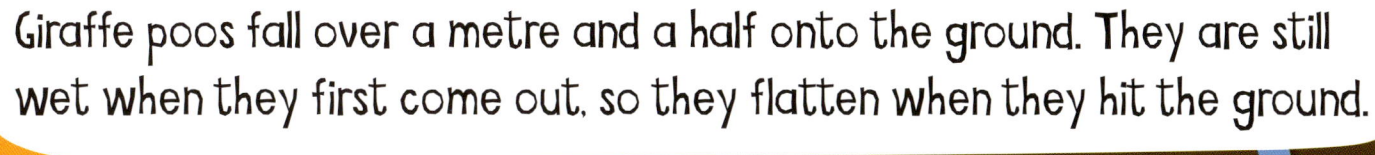
Giraffe poos fall over a metre and a half onto the ground. They are still wet when they first come out, so they flatten when they hit the ground.

Giraffes eat lots of leaves. Once they have swallowed their food, they bring it back up again later and chew it to make it easier to digest.

BONUS POO!

PICK YOUR OWN POO

Dung beetles roll other animals' poo to their homes to lay their eggs in. When their eggs hatch, the baby beetles feed off the poo.

"The kids will love this!"

A dung beetle can roll a ball that is more than twice its height!

POOING YOUR PANTS

Vultures will poo and wee all over their own legs. This might sound disgusting and dirty, but their waste actually helps to kill any nasty bacteria they might have stepped in.

Pooing and weeing on themselves also helps vultures to keep cool on the hot savannah.

I'm out of soap – does anyone need a poo?

GLOSSARY

bacteria	tiny living things, too small to see, that live inside some animals
calcium	something that is in teeth, bones and shells that makes these things hard and strong
carnivores	animals that eat other animals instead of plants
communal	shared or used by a group or community
digest	to break down food into things that can be used by the body
herbivore	an animal that only eats plants
pack	a group of the same animal (for example, wolves)
prey	animals that are eaten by other animals for food
savannah	a large area of flat land with grass and very few trees
territory	an area that an animal thinks to be its own
vegetation	different types of plants including grass, bushes and trees
wallow	to roll around in mud, sand or water to keep cool or stay away from insects

INDEX

babies 17, 22
carnivores 12-13, 23
chewing 18, 21
eating 6, 12-14, 16-17, 20-22

grass 7, 14
herbivores 14, 16-18, 20-21
scavengers 12, 23
teeth 13

tongues 20
wallowing 7, 9
water 6-7, 9